NEWPORT · CHEI
CAERLEON

CW00327709

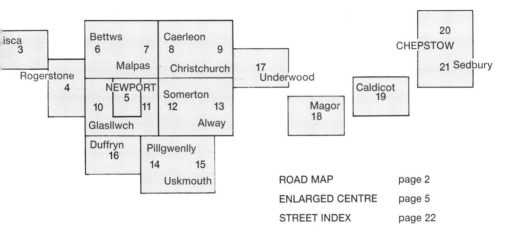

ROAD MAP   page 2

ENLARGED CENTRE   page 5

STREET INDEX   page 22

Car Park	P
Public Convenience	C
Place of Worship	+
One-way Street	→
Pedestrianized	
Post Office	●

Scale of street plans 4 inches to 1 mile
Unless otherwise stated

eet plans prepared and published by ESTATE PUBLICATIONS, Bridewell House, TENTERDEN, KENT.
The Publishers acknowledge the co-operation of the local authorities
of towns represented in this atlas.

Ordnance Survey® This product includes mapping data licensed from Ordnance Survey®
with the permission of the Controller of Her Majesty's Stationery Office.

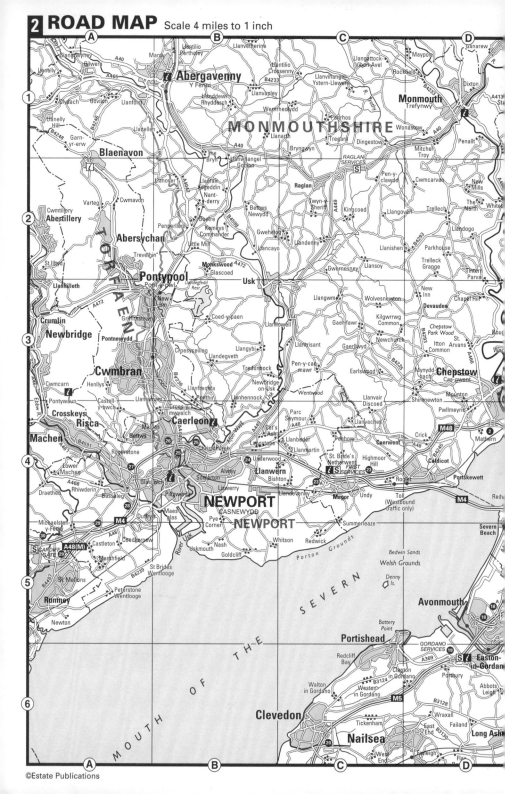

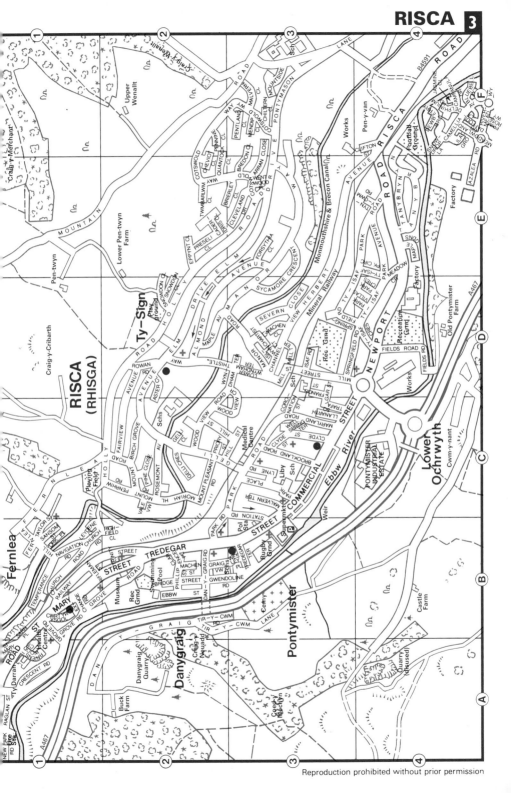

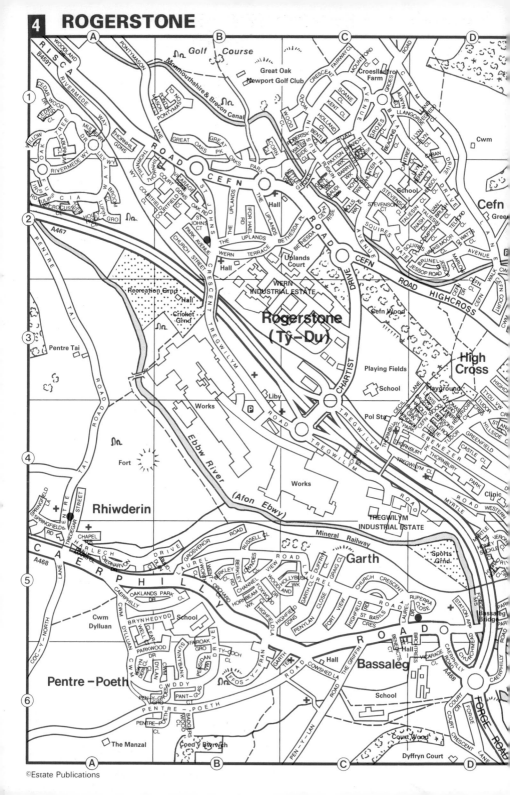

4 ROGERSTONE

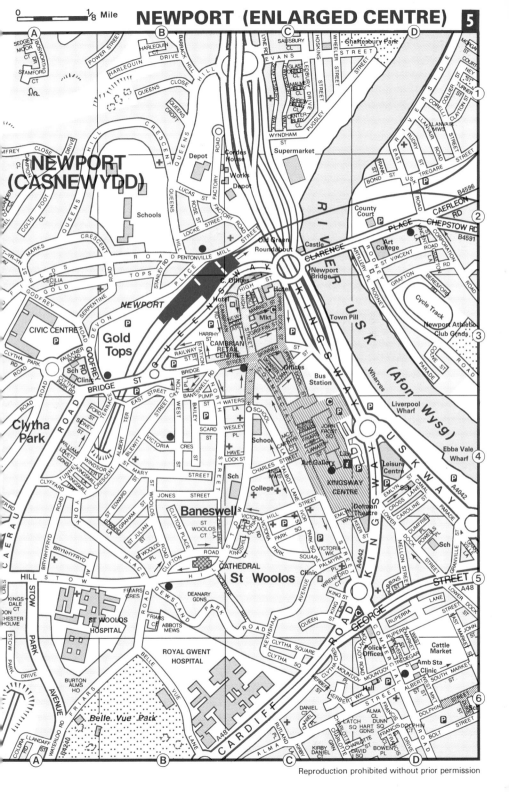

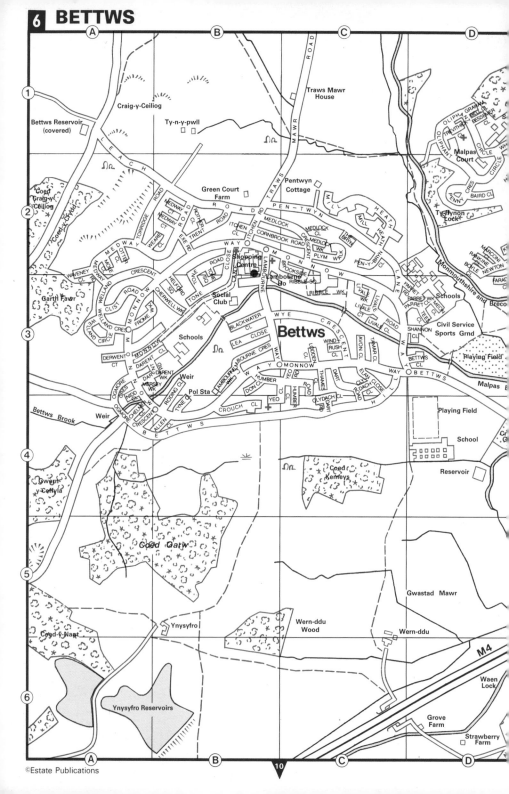

Traws Mawr House

Craig-y-Ceiliog

Bettws Reservoir (covered)

Ty-n-y-pwll

Pentwyn Cottage

Coed Craig-y-Ceiliog

Coed-y-Cryd

Green Court Farm

Malpas Court

Ty Mynon Lock

Monmouthshire and Breco

Garth Fawr

Shopping Centre

Lambourne Ho

Schools

Social Club

Schools

Bettws

Civil Service Sports Grnd

Playing Field

Malpas

Weir

Pol Sta

Bettws Brook

Weir

Playing Field

School

Gwern-y-Ceffyla

Coed Kemeys

Reservoir

Coed Garw

Gwastad Mawr

Ynysyfro

Wern-ddu Wood

Wern-ddu

Coed-y-Nant

M4

Waen Lock

Ynysyfro Reservoirs

Grove Farm

Strawberry Farm

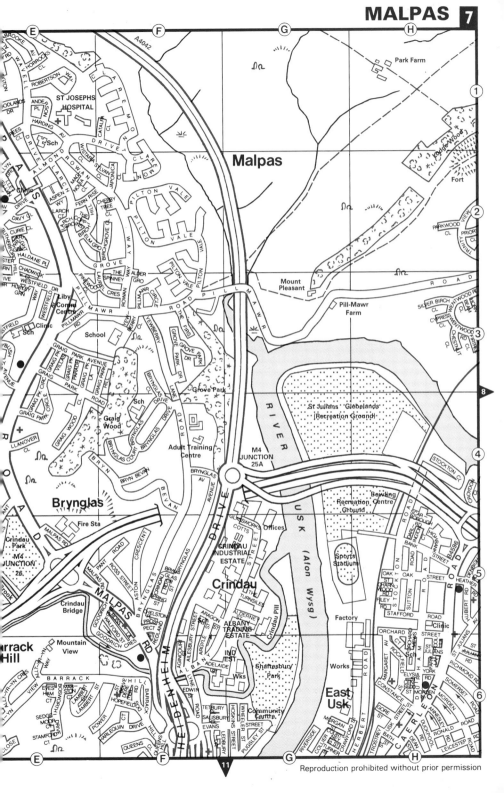

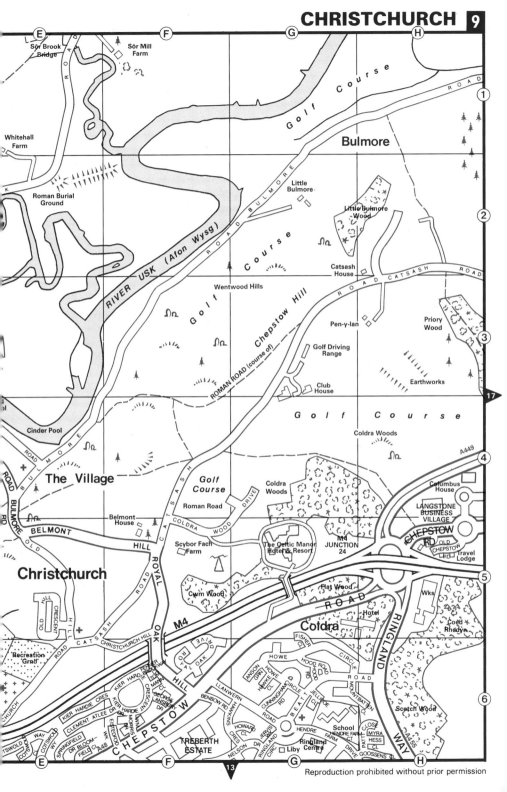

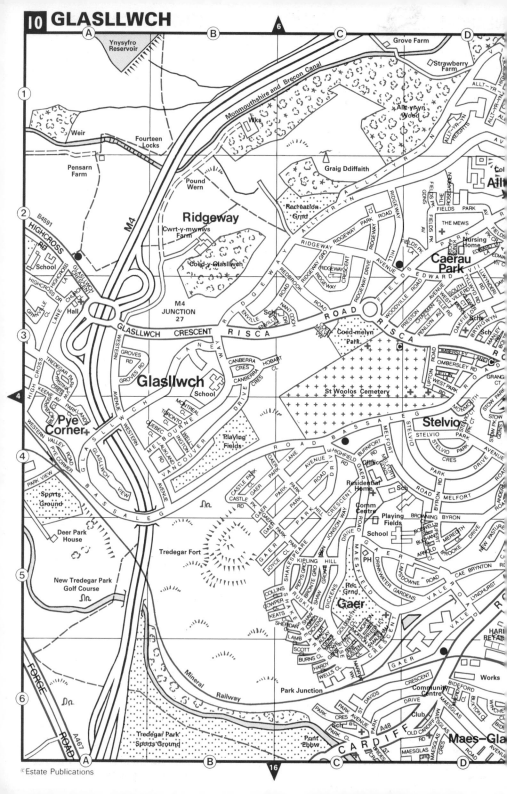

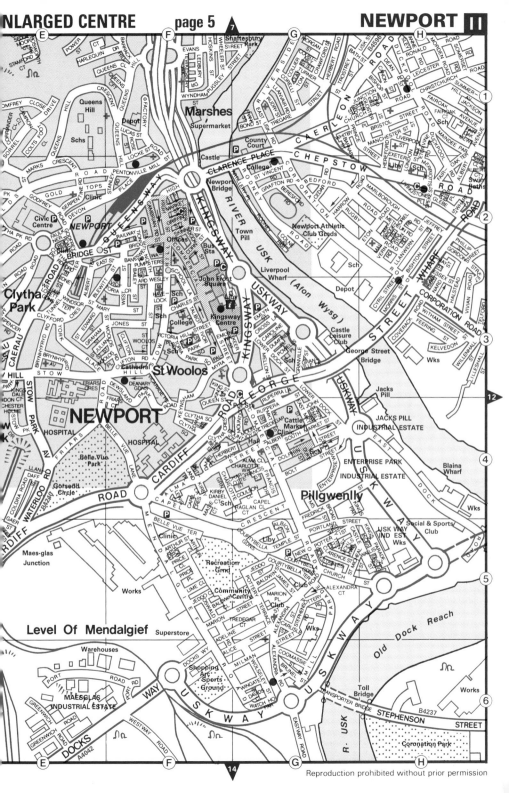

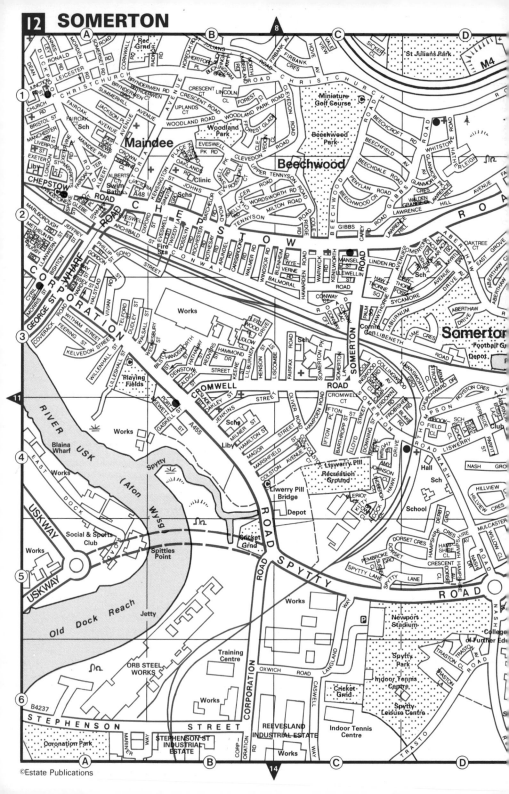

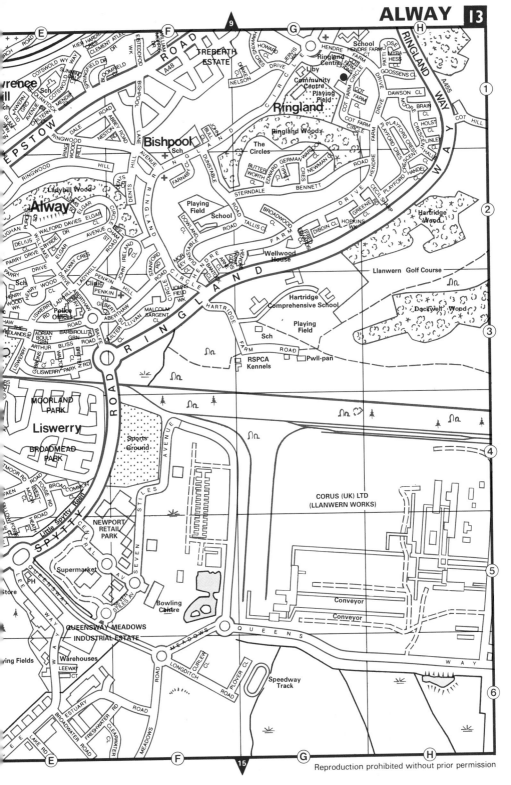

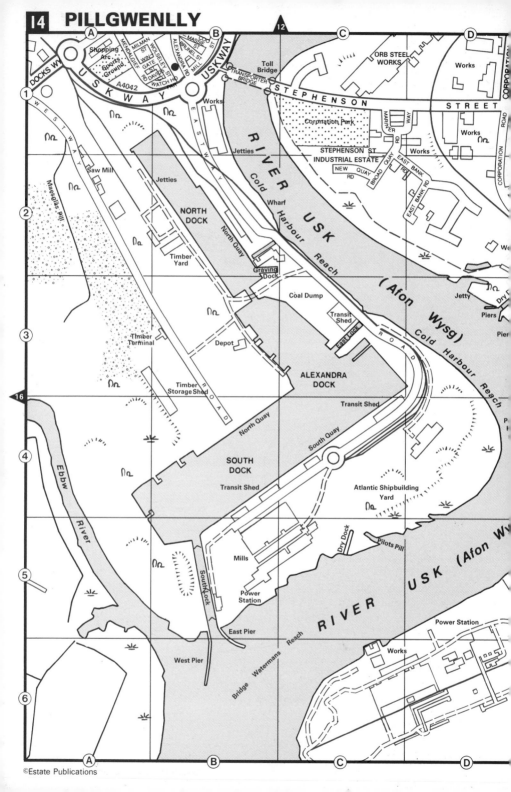

14 PILLGWENLLY

©Estate Publications

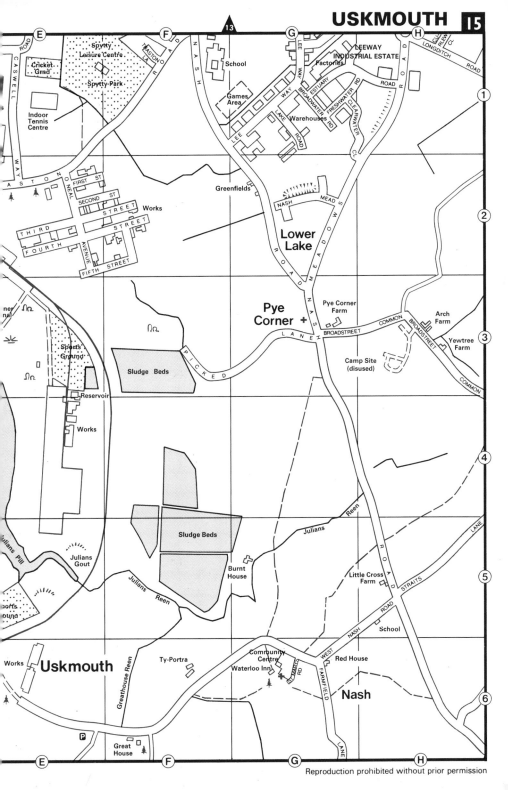

E
F
13
G
H

Spytty Leisure Centre
Cricket Grnd
Spytty Park
Indoor Tennis Centre

CASWELL ROAD
ASTON WAY
NEAL
FIRST ST
SECOND ST
STREET
THIRD
FOURTH
AVENUE
FIFTH STREET

Works

School
Games Area
Warehouses
Factories

LEEWAY INDUSTRIAL ESTATE
LONGDITCH ROAD
LEE WAY
BROADWATERS WAY
LAKE ROAD
ESTUARY WAY
FRESHWATER RD
CLEARWATER CL
ROAD

Greenfields
NASH
Lower Lake
NASH MEADOWS ROAD

ner nal
Sports Ground
Sludge Beds
Reservoir
Works
Julians Pill
Julians Gout
Sludge Beds
orts ouna

Pye Corner +
PICKED LANE
NASH ROAD
BROADSTREET
COMMON
BROADSTREET
COMMON

Pye Corner Farm
Camp Site (disused)
Arch Farm
Yewtree Farm

Julians
Reen
Julians Reen
Burnt House
Little Cross Farm
ROAD
STRAITS
LANE
School

Works
Uskmouth
Ty-Portra
Greathouse Reen
Community Centre
Waterloo Inn
Red House
NASH WEST RD
FARMFIELD
Nash

P
Great House

E
F
G
H
LANE

1
2
3
4
5
6

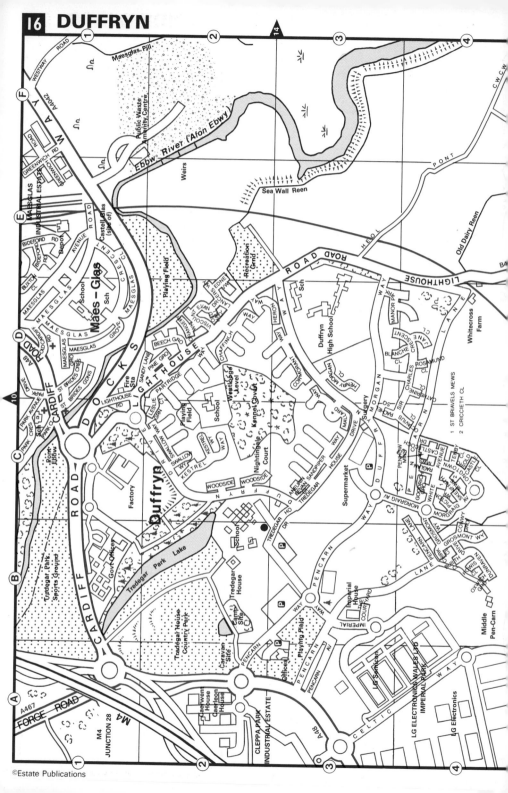

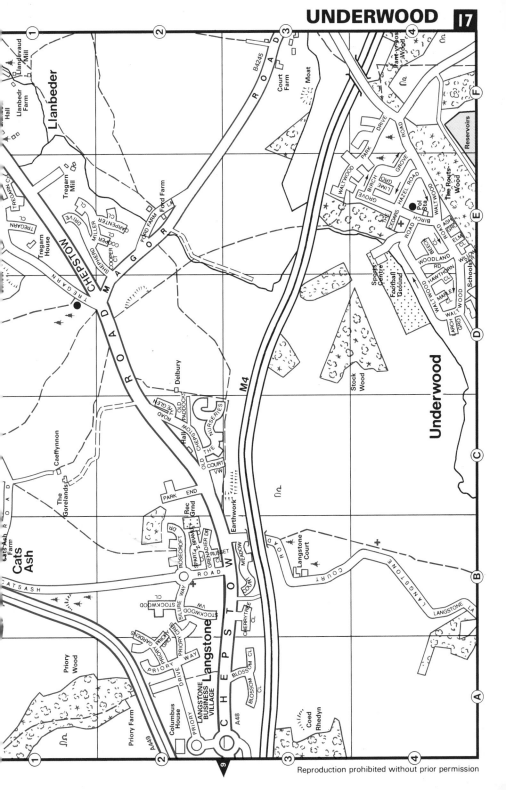

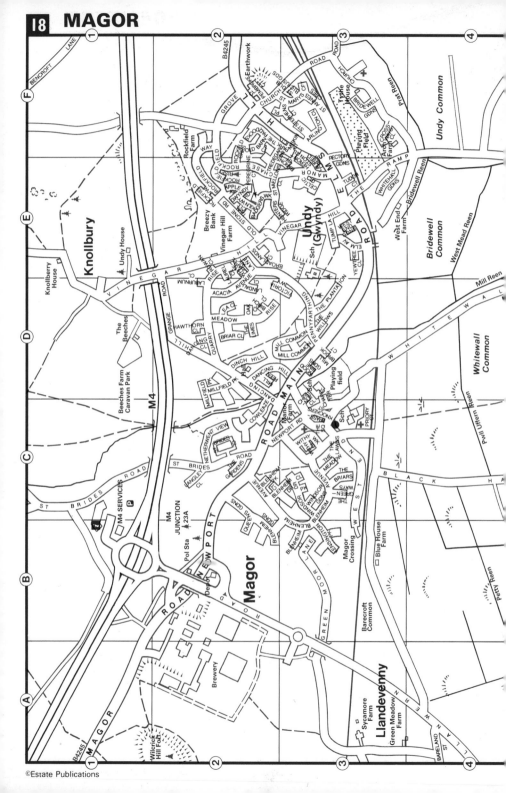

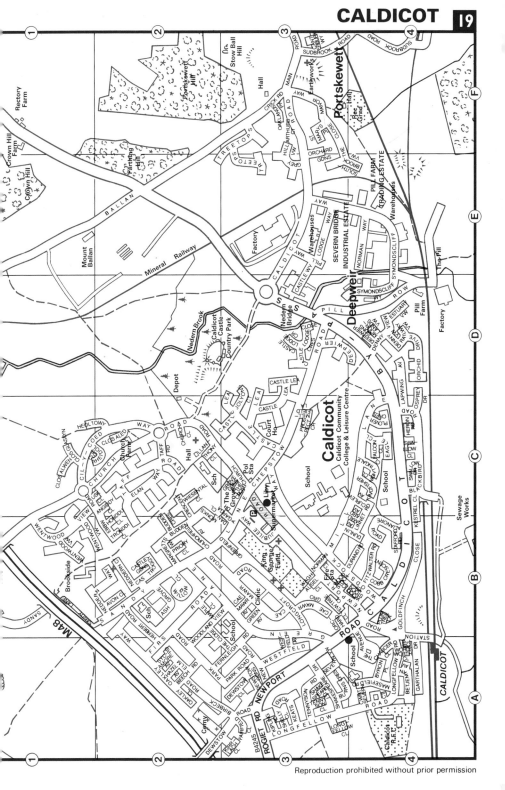

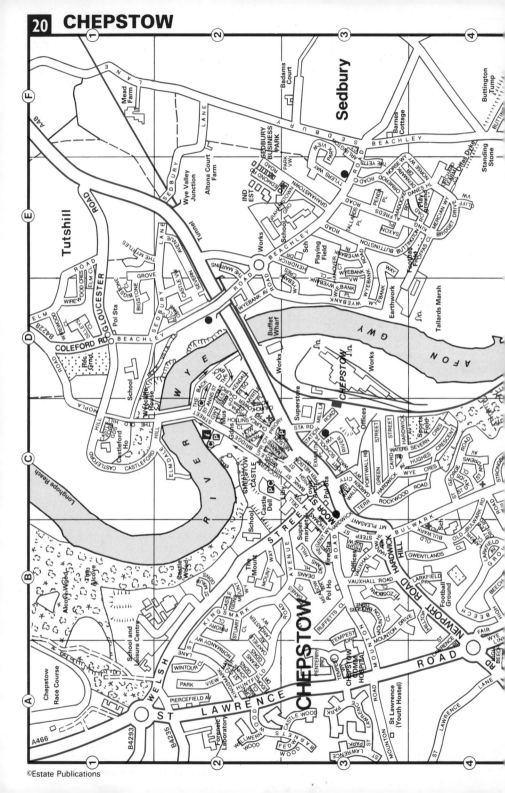

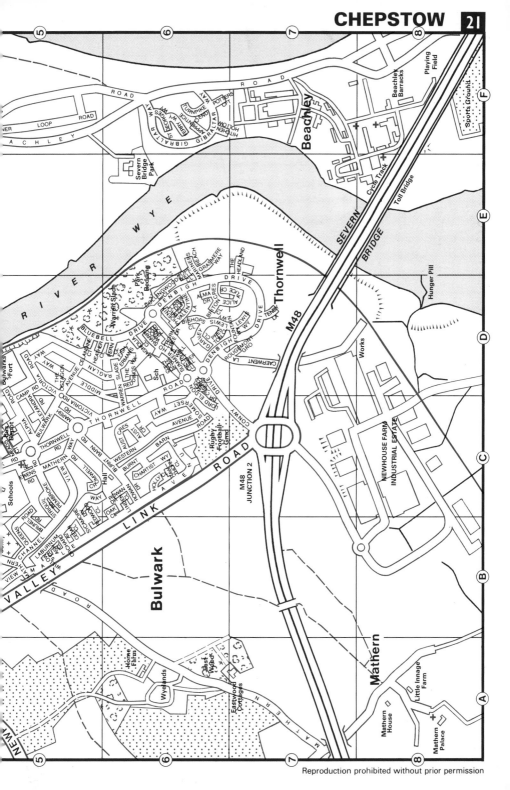

A - Z INDEX TO STREETS
with Postcodes

The Index includes some names for which there is insufficient space on the maps. These names are preceded by an * and are followed by the nearest adjoining thoroughfare.

NEWPORT

22

Farm Circle. NP19 13 G1
Farm Clo. NP19 13 G1
Farm Gdns. NP19 13 G1
Hill. NP18 13 H1
nan Clo. NP19 8 C6
swold Clo,
otswold Way. NP19 13 E1
wold Way. NP19 13 E1
son Clo. NP20 11 G4
rt Cres. NP10 4 D6
rt Gdns. NP10 4 B2
rt Meadow. NP18 17 B3
rt View. NP18 17 C2
rtfield Clo. NP10 4 B2
rtney St. NP19 11 G1
rtybella Gdns. NP20 11 G5
rtybella Ter. NP10 11 G5
erack Rd. NP19 11 H3
per Clo. NP20 10 C5
vshed La. NP10 4 C6
wford St. NP19 11 G1
scent Ct. NP19 12 B1
scent Rd. NP19 12 B1
cieth Clo. NP10 16 V4
dau Rd. NP20 7 F5
cus Clo. NP10 4 A2
mwell Ct. NP19 12 C3
mwell Rd. NP19 12 B3
ss La. NP20 5 D4
ss St. NP19 8 D3
ich Clo. NP20 6 B4
own Arcade,
High St. NP20 5 C3
wn Clo. NP18 8 D3
wn St. NP19 12 A1
ydon Clo. NP19 8 A4
iberland Rd. NP19 8 A4
ningham Rd. NP19 9 G6
e Clo. NP20 7 E2
ew Clo. NP19 13 F6
ter Clo. NP19 8 A4
n Cwddy Dri. NP10 4 A6
n Dylan Clo. NP10 4 B6
n Dylluan. NP10 4 A5
n La. NP10 4 C1
ress Clo. NP18 8 A3
I St. NP19 11 H3

e Rd. NP19 13 E1
iel Ct. NP19 5 C6
iel Pl. NP20 5 C6
ent Clo. NP20 6 A3
ent Rd. NP20 6 A3
ent Walk. NP20 6 B3
ington Ct. NP19 7 H5
t Rd. NP20 6 C3
win Dri. NP20 6 D2
id Sq. NP20 5 D6
id Walk. NP10 4 D4
y Clo. NP20 7 E2
vson Clo. NP19 13 H1
n St. NP19 11 H1
nery Gdns. NP20 5 B5
us Clo. NP19 13 E2
ibigh Rd. NP19 8 A5
ts Clo. NP19 13 F2
ts Hill. NP19 13 F2
by Gro. NP19 12 D5
went Ct. NP20 6 A3
on Ct. NP18 8 B1
on Pl. NP20 5 A3
vsland Park Rd.
P20 5 B5
vstow St. NP19 12 B3
din Clo. NP19 13 G2
kens Dri. NP20 10 C5
kpool Rd. NP19 11 H1
lley St. NP19 12 A3
fryn Clo. NP10 4 C5
fryn Dri. NP10 16 C3
fryn Way. NP10 16 C3

Duke St. NP20 5 D6
Dumfries Pl. NP20 5 D5
Dunn Sq. NP20 5 D6
Dunraven Dri. NP10 16 B4
Dunstable Rd. NP19 13 F2
Durham Rd. NP19 7 H6

East Bank Rd. NP19 14 D2
East Dock Rd. NP20 11 H4
East Grove Rd. NP19 12 D2
East Lynne Gdns. NP18 8 D2
East Market St. NP20 5 D5
East St. NP20 5 B4
East Usk Rd. NP19 5 D2
Eastfield Dri. NP18 8 B1
Eastfield Mews. NP18 8 C1
Eastfield Rd. NP18 8 B1
Eastfield View. NP18 8 C1
Eastfield Way. NP18 8 C1
Eastmoor Rd. NP19 13 E4
Eastway Rd. NP19 14 B1
Ebenezer Dri. NP10 4 D4
Edison Ridge. NP20 7 E2
Edney View. NP10 16 D2
Edward German Cres.
  NP19 13 G2
Edward La. NP20 5 B5
Edward VII Av. NP20 10 D2
Edward VII Cres. NP20 10 D2
Edward VII La. NP20 10 D2
Edwin St. NP20 7 F6
Eisteddfod Walk. NP19 13 F1
Elaine Cres. NP19 8 A5
Elan Clo. NP20 6 C3
Elder Clo. NP18 8 A3
Elgar Av. NP19 13 E2
Elgar Circle. NP19 13 E2
Elgar Clo. NP19 13 E2
Elm Clo. NP18 17 E4
Elm Gro. NP20 7 E2
Elysia St. NP19 7 H6
Emlyn St. NP20 5 D4
Emlyn Walk. NP20 5 C4
Ennerdale Ct. NP19 8 A5
Enterprise Way. NP20 11 G4
Enville Clo. NP20 10 B3
Enville Rd. NP20 10 B3
Eschol Clo. NP19 12 D4
Essex Ct. NP18 8 B1
Essex St. NP19 12 A3
Estuary Rd. NP19 15 G1
Eton Rd. NP19 11 H2
Evans St. NP20 5 C1
*Evergreen, Stow
  Park Circle. NP20 10 D4
Evesham Ct. NP20 7 E6
Eveswell Ct. NP19 12 A2
Eveswell Park Rd. NP19 12 B1
Eveswell St. NP19 12 B2
Exe Rd. NP20 6 B2
Exeter Rd. NP19 11 H1
Exeter St. NP19 11 H2

Factory Rd. NP20 5 B2
Fairfax Rd. NP19 12 C3
Fairfield Clo. NP18 8 B2
Fairfield Rd. NP18 8 B2
Fairoak Av. NP19 12 A1
Fairoak Ct. NP19 12 A1
Fairoak Gro. NP10 4 B5
Fairoak Mews. NP19 12 A1
Fairoak Ter. NP19 11 H2
Fairway Clo. NP10 4 C1
Fallowfield Dri. NP19 13 E4
Faraday Clo. NP20 6 D3
Farm La. NP19 7 H6
Farmfield La. NP18 15 G6
Farmwood Clo. NP19 12 D2
Farnaby Clo. NP19 13 F2
Faulkner Rd. NP20 5 A3
Feering St. NP19 11 H3
Fenner Brockway Clo.
  NP19 9 F6
Fern Rise. NP20 7 E2
Fernside. NP19 12 D4
Fforest Glade. NP19 12 B1
Ffos-y-Fran. NP10 4 B6
Fields Park Av. NP20 10 D2
Fields Park Cres. NP20 10 D2
Fields Park Gdns. NP20 10 D2
Fields Park La. NP20 10 D2
Fields Park Rd. NP20 10 C3
Fields Rd. NP20 5 A3
Fifth St. NP19 15 E2
Filey Rd. NP19 7 H5

Firbank Av. NP19 8 B6
Firbank Cres. NP19 8 B6
First St. NP19 15 E2
Firtree Clo. NP18 8 A3
Fisher Clo. NP19 9 G6
Fleetwood Clo. NP19 12 B3
Fleming Clo. NP20 7 E2
Flint Clo. NP19 8 C6
Flint Ct. NP18 8 B1
Ford Farm La. NP18 17 E2
Ford St. NP20 5 A4
Forest Clo. NP19 12 B1
Forge Clo. NP18 8 D1
Forge La. NP10 4 D6
Forge Mews. NP10 4 D5
Forge Rd. NP10 4 D6
Fort View. NP10 4 C5
Fosse Clo. NP19 13 E5
Fosse La. NP18 8 C3
Fosse Rd. NP19 13 E4
Fourth St. NP19 15 E2
Foxwood Clo. NP10 4 B5
Francis Clo. NP20 5 D6
Francis Clo. NP20 5 D6
Francis St. NP20 5 D6
Frank St. NP19 5 D2
Fred Edwards Clo.
  NP19 13 G2
Frederick Mews. NP20 11 G4
Frederick St. NP20 11 G4
Freshwater Rd. NP19 15 G1
Friars Ct. NP20 5 B5
Friars Cres. NP20 5 B5
Friars Rd. NP20 5 A6
Friars St. NP20 5 C4
Frobisher Rd. NP19 12 C4
Frome Walk. NP20 6 A3
Fuscia Way. NP10 4 A2

Gaer Park Av. NP20 10 B4
Gaer Park Dri. NP20 10 B4
Gaer Park Hill. NP20 10 B4
Gaer Park La. NP20 10 B4
Gaer Park Par. NP20 10 B5
Gaer Park Rd. NP20 10 B5
Gaer Rd. NP20 10 C4
Gaer St. NP20 11 E5
Gaer Vale. NP20 10 D5
Gainsborough Dri. NP19 8 B5
Garth Clo. NP10 4 C6
Garth Ter. NP10 4 C6
Gaskell St. NP19 12 B4
Gaudi Walk. NP10 4 C2
George Lansbury Dri.
  NP19 9 F6
George St. NP20 5 D5
Gibbons Clo. NP19 13 E3
Gibbs Rd. NP19 12 C2
Gilbert Clo. NP19 13 F3
Glanmor Cres. NP19 12 D2
Glanmor Park Av. NP19 12 D2
Glanwern Av. NP19 13 E1
Glanwern Clo. NP19 13 E1
Glanwern Dri. NP19 13 E1
Glanwern Gro. NP19 13 E1
Glanwern Rise. NP19 13 E1
Glasllwch Cres. NP20 10 A3
Glasllwch La. NP20 10 A4
Glasllwch View. NP20 10 A4
Glassworks Cotts. NP20 7 G5
Glastonbury Clo. NP20 5 C1
Glebe St. NP19 11 H2
Glen Usk View. NP19 8 C1
Gloster Pl. NP19 11 H1
Gloster St. NP19 11 H1
*Gloucester Ct,
  Roman Way. NP18 8 B1
Godfrey Rd. NP20 5 A3
Gold Tops. NP20 5 A3
Goldcroft Common.
  NP18 8 D3
*Goldcroft Ct,
  Church St. NP18 8 D3
Goldsmith Clo. NP20 10 C5
Goodrich Cres. NP20 7 E5
Goodrich Gro. NP10 16 C4
Goossens Clo. NP19 13 H1
Gordon St. NP19 12 A2
Gore St. NP19 7 H6
Goya Clo. NP19 8 B6
Grafton La. NP19 5 D2
Grafton Rd. NP19 5 D3
Graham Bell Clo. NP20 6 D1
Graham St. NP20 5 A3
Graig Clo. NP10 4 C5
Graig Park Av. NP19 7 E3

Graig Park Circle. NP20 7 E4
Graig Park Hill. NP20 7 E3
Graig Park La. NP20 7 E3
Graig Park Par. NP20 7 E3
Graig Park Rd. NP20 7 E3
Graig Park Villas. NP20 7 E3
Graig Wood Clo. NP20 7 E4
Grange Ct. NP20 10 D3
Granville Clo. NP10 4 D4
Granville La. NP20 5 D5
Granville St. NP20 5 D5
Great Oaks Pk. NP10 4 A3
Greene Clo. NP19 13 G2
Greenfield. NP18 8 B2
Greenfield Rd. NP10 4 D4
Greenmeadow Av.
  NP19 12 D4
Greenmeadow Rd.
  NP19 12 D4
Greenwich Rd. NP20 11 E6
Grenadier Dri. NP18 17 B2
Griffin St. NP20 5 C3
Grindale Walk. NP10 4 C2
Groes Clo. NP10 4 C1
Groes Rd. NP10 4 C1
Grosmont Way. NP10 16 B4
Grosvenor Rd. NP10 4 B5
Grove Park Dri. NP20 7 F3
Groves Rd. NP20 10 A3
Gwladys Pl. NP18 8 C2

Hadrian Clo. NP18 8 B1
*Hafod Ct, Stow Park
  Cres. NP20 10 D4
Haisbro Av. NP19 8 A4
Haldane Pl. NP20 7 E2
Halle Clo. NP19 13 H2
Halstead St. NP19 12 A3
Hamilton St. NP19 12 B4
Hammond Dri. NP19 12 B3
Hampden Rd. NP19 12 C4
Hampshire Av. NP19 12 D5
Hampshire Clo. NP19 12 D5
Hampshire Cres. NP19 12 D5
Hanbury Clo. NP18 8 D3
Handel Clo. NP19 13 H2
Handsworth St. NP19 12 B3
Harding Av. NP20 7 E1
Hardy Clo. NP20 10 C6
Hargreaves Dri. NP20 6 D2
Harlech Dri. NP10 4 A5
Harlequin Ct. NP20 5 B1
Harlequin Dri. NP20 5 B1
Harold Walk. NP10 4 D4
Harrhy St. NP20 5 B3
*Harrogate Rd,
  Scarborough Rd,
  NP19 7 H5
Harrow Clo. NP18 8 A1
Harrow Rd. NP19 11 G2
Hart Gdns. NP20 5 D6
Hartridge Farm Rd.
  NP19 13 F3
Harvey Clo. NP20 7 E2
Hathaway St. NP19 12 B3
Hatherleigh. NP19 12 D1
Havelock St. NP20 5 C4
Hawarden Rd. NP19 12 C3
Hawke Clo. NP19 9 G6
Hawkins Cres. NP19 9 G6
Hawksmoor Clo. NP10 4 D2
Hawksworth Gro. NP19 12 D3
Hawthorn Clo. NP18 17 D4
Hawthorne Av. NP19 12 C3
Hawthorne Fosse. NP19 12 C3
Hawthorne Sq. NP19 12 C3
Hayling Clo. NP19 8 B6
*Haynes Ct,
  James St. NP20 11 G5
Hazel Rd. NP18 17 E4
Hazel Walk. NP18 8 A3
Hazlitt Clo. NP20 10 C6
Heath Clo. NP19 13 E5
Heather Rd. NP19 8 A5
Heidenheim Dri. NP20 7 F6
Helford Sq. NP20 6 B3
Hendre Farm Ct. NP19 13 G1
Hendre Farm Dri. NP19 13 F2
Hendre Farm Gdns.
  NP19 13 G2
Henry Morgan Clo.
  NP10 16 D3
Henry Wood Clo. NP19 13 E3
Henry Wood Wk. NP19 13 E3
Hensol Clo. NP10 4 D2
Henson St. NP19 12 B3

Heol Pont Cwcw. NP10 16 E3
Herbert Rd. NP19 11 G1
Herbert St. NP20 5 C6
Herbert Walk. NP20 5 C6
Hereford Ct. NP18 8 C1
Hereford St. NP19 11 H1
Heron Way. NP10 16 D2
Hertford Pl. NP19 8 B6
High St, Caerleon. NP18 8 D3
High St, Newport. NP20 5 C3
Highbank. NP19 7 H5
Highcroft Rd. NP20 10 D1
High Cross La. NP10 10 A3
Highcross Clo. NP10 4 D4
Highcross Dri. NP10 10 A3
Highcross Rd. NP10 4 D3
Highcross Rd. NP10 10 C4
Highfield Clo. NP18 8 B1
Highfield Gdns. NP10 4 C5
Highfield Rd,
  Bassaleg. NP10 4 C5
Highfield Rd,
  Caerleon. NP18 8 B1
Highfield Rd,
  Newport. NP20 10 C4
Highfield Way. NP18 8 B1
Hill St. NP20 5 C4
Hilla Rd. NP20 11 E3
Hillcrest. NP18 8 B1
Hillside Cres. NP10 4 D4
Hillview Cres. NP19 12 D4
Hobart Clo. NP20 10 B3
Hogarth Clo. NP19 8 B5
Holbein Rd. NP19 8 C6
Holland Clo. NP10 4 C1
Hollybush Av. NP20 7 E3
Hollybush Clo. NP20 7 E3
Hollybush Walk. NP10 4 C5
Hollyhock Clo. NP10 4 A2
Holst Clo. NP19 13 H1
Home Farm Clo. NP18 8 B3
Home Farm Cres. NP18 8 B3
Home Farm Grn. NP18 8 B2
Honeysuckle Clo. NP10 4 D5
Hood Rd. NP19 9 G6
Hopefield. NP20 7 F6
Hopkins Walk. NP19 13 G2
Hornbeam Clo. NP18 8 A3
Hornbeam Walk. NP10 4 B5
Horrocks Clo. NP20 7 E1
Hoskins St. NP20 5 C1
Hove Av. NP18 8 C6
Howard Clo. NP19 9 G6
Howe Circle. NP19 9 G6
Hubert Rise. NP10 4 D4
Hubert Rd. NP19 8 A5
Humber Clo. NP20 6 C3
Humber Rd. NP20 6 B3
Hunter Clo. NP10 4 C2
Huxley Grn. NP20 7 E3
Hydrangea Clo. NP10 4 D5

Ifor Hael Rd. NP10 4 B2
Ifton Pl. NP19 12 C4
Ifton Rd. NP19 12 C4
Imperial Way. NP10 16 B3
INDUSTRIAL & RETAIL:
  Albany
    Trading Est. NP20 7 G5
  Cambrian
    Retail Centre. NP20 5 B3
  Cleppa Park Ind Est.
    NP10 16 A2
  Crindau Ind. NP20 7 F5
  Enterprise Park
    Ind Est. NP20 11 G4
  Harlech Retail Pk.
    NP20 10 D5
  Jacks Pill Ind Est.
    NP20 11 H4
  Langstone Business
    Village. NP18 17 A2
  Leeway Ind Est.
    NP19 15 G1
  Maesglas Ind Est.
    NP20 11 E6
  Newport Retail Pk.
    NP19 13 E5
  Orb Steel Works.
    NP19 12 A6
  Queensway Meadows
    Ind Est. NP19 13 E5
  Reevesland Ind Est.
    NP19 12 B6
  Stephenson St Ind Est.
    NP19 12 B6

23

ourn Clo. NP19 8 C6
lan Ct. NP20 11 G4
lan Mews. NP10 16 C4
way St. NP20 5 B3
way Ter. NP18 8 D2
nsey Clo. NP19 8 B6
kine Clo. NP20 6 D2
hael Clo. NP19 8 B6
brook Rd. NP20 10 C2
land St. NP20 7 F6
vers St. NP19 12 B3
wood Clo. NP18 8 A3
ne Ct. NP19 12 C4
s Clo. NP20 7 E1
nbrandt Way. NP19 8 B5
oir Rd. NP19 8 C5
ervoir Clo. NP10 4 D4
nolds Clo. NP19 8 B5
ddlan Clo. NP10 4 B5
ole Sq. NP20 6 C3
ole Walk. NP20 6 C3
mond Rd. NP19 8 A6
geway. NP20 10 B3
geway Av. NP20 10 C2
geway Clo. NP20 10 C2
geway Ct. NP20 10 C2
geway Cres. NP20 10 C2
geway Dri. NP20 10 C3
geway Gro. NP20 10 C2
geway Hill. NP20 10 C2
geway Park Rd. P20 10 C2
gland Circle. NP19 13 F2
ngland Ho, Ringland Circle. NP19 13 F2
ngland Pl, Ringland Circle. NP19 13 F2
gland Way. NP19 13 F3
gwood Av. NP19 13 E1
gwood Hill. NP19 13 E2
ca Rd, Basllwch. NP20 10 B3
ca Rd, Rogerstone. NP10 4 A1
er View. NP19 8 A4
erside. NP19 5 D1
bins St. NP20 5 D5
ert Clo. NP20 11 F5
erts Clo. NP10 4 C1
ertson Way. NP20 7 E1
hester Rd. NP19 12 B2
kfield St. NP19 7 H6
ling Clo. NP20 6 B4
dney Par. NP19 5 D3
dney Rd. NP19 5 D2
's Walk. NP10 4 C2
nan Gates. NP18 8 D3
nan Reach. NP18 8 A3
nan Rd. NP18 17 A1
nan Way. NP18 8 B1
nney Clo. NP19 8 C6
ald Rd. NP19 12 A1
samund Clo. NP10 16 D4
e St. NP20 5 B2
secroft Dri. NP18 17 B2
endale Ct. NP19 12 B2
ss La. NP20 7 F5
ss St. NP20 7 F5
sslyn Rd. NP19 12 B2
her Clo. NP20 6 B2
hesay Rd. NP19 12 B2
wan Way. NP20 7 E2
val Oak Dri. NP18 9 F5
val Oak Hill. NP18 9 F5
yce Walk. NP10 4 C2
yston Cres. NP19 12 D3
bens Clo. NP19 8 B5
dry St. NP19 5 D1
gby Rd. NP19 11 G2
perra Clo. NP10 4 D5
perra La. NP20 5 D5
perra St. NP20 5 D5
pert Brooke Dri. P20 10 D5
skin Av. NP10 4 C1
skin Rise. NP20 10 C5
ssell Clo. NP10 4 B5
ssell Dri. NP20 7 E2
ssell Dri Gdns. NP20 7 E3
sset Clo. NP18 17 B2
herford Hill. NP20 7 E2
land Pl. NP20 5 C6

Annes Clo. NP10 4 D4
St Annes Cres. NP19 8 A6
St Basils Cres. NP10 4 C5
St Benedicts Ct. NP10 4 C5
St Briavels Mews. NP10 16 C4
St Brides Cres. NP20 16 D1
St Brides Gdns. NP20 16 D1
St Cadocs Clo. NP18 8 C2
St Cecilia Ct. NP20 5 A3
St Davids Clo. NP20 11 G6
St Davids Cres. NP20 10 C6
St Edward St. NP20 5 B4
St Georges Cres. NP19 8 A6
St Johns Ct. NP10 4 B2
St Johns Cres. NP10 4 B2
St Johns Rd. NP19 12 B2
St Julian St. NP20 5 B5
St Julians Av. NP19 8 A6
St Julians Ct. NP19 7 H6
St Julians Rd. NP19 8 A6
St Marks Cres. NP20 5 A2
St Mary St. NP20 5 B4
St Marys Rd. NP18 15 G6
St Merriotts Pl. NP19 11 H2
St Michael St. NP20 11 G5
*St Michaels Ct, Church St. NP20 11 G5
St Michaels Mews. NP20 11 G5
St Stephens Rd. NP20 11 G5
St Vincent Ct, St Vincent La. NP19 5 D2
St Vincent La. NP19 5 D2
St Vincent Rd. NP19 5 D2
St Woolos Ct. NP20 5 B5
St Woolos Pl. NP20 5 B5
St Woolos Rd. NP20 5 B4
Salisbury Clo. NP19 5 C1
Sandpiper Way. NP10 16 C3
Sandy La. NP10 16 D1
Scarborough Rd. NP19 7 H5
Scard St. NP20 5 B4
School Ct. NP19 12 D4
School La. NP20 5 C4
Scott Clo. NP20 10 C6
Scott Walk. NP10 4 C1
Second St. NP19 15 E2
Sedgemoor Ct. NP20 7 E6
Serpentine Rd. NP20 5 A3
Seven Stiles Av. NP19 13 F5
*Shaftesbury Ct, Evans St. NP20 5 C1
*Shaftesbury St, Evans St. NP20 5 C1
Shaftesbury Walk. NP20 5 C1
Shakespeare Cres. NP20 10 C5
Shannon Clo. NP20 6 D3
Shaw Gro. NP20 10 C5
*Shea Gdns, Bown Pl. NP20 5 D6
Shelley Rd. NP19 12 B2
Shepherd Dri. NP18 17 E2
Sheridan Clo. NP20 10 C5
Shetland Clo. NP19 8 B6
Shetland Walk. NP19 8 B6
Shrewsbury Clo. NP20 5 C1
Sickert Clo. NP19 8 C6
Sidney St. NP20 5 A4
Silure Way. NP20 17 B2
Silver Fir Sq. NP10 4 D5
Silverbirch Clo. NP18 8 A3
Simpson Clo. NP20 6 D2
Sims Sq. NP19 13 E2
Sir Charles Cres. NP10 16 C3
Skenfrith Mews. NP10 16 C4
Skinner La. NP20 5 C3
Skinner St. NP20 5 C3
Skinners Row. NP19 13 E3
Slade St. NP19 12 B4
Soane Clo. NP10 4 C1
Soho St. NP19 12 A2
Somerset Rd. NP19 12 A1
Somerton Cres. NP19 12 D2
Somerton La. NP19 12 C3
Somerton Pk. NP19 12 C3
Somerton Rd. NP19 12 C3
Sorrel Dri. NP20 5 A2
South Market St. NP20 5 D6
Southville Rd. NP20 10 D3
Spartan Clo. NP18 17 B2
Speke St. NP19 11 H2
Spencer Rd. NP20 5 A4
Spring St. NP20 7 F5
Springfield Dri. NP19 13 E1
Springfield La. NP10 4 A4
Springfield Rd. NP10 4 A3
Spytty La. NP19 12 C5
Spytty Rd. NP19 12 C5
Squires Clo. NP10 4 D2
Squires Gate. NP10 4 C2
Stafford Rd. NP19 7 H5
Stamford Ct. NP20 7 E6
Stanford Rd. NP19 13 F2
Stanley Rd. NP20 5 B3
Station App, Bassaleg. NP10 4 D5
Station App, Caerleon. NP18 8 D2
Station Rd. NP18 8 D2
Station St. NP20 5 B3
Steer Cres. NP19 8 C6
Stelvio Park Av. NP20 10 D4
Stelvio Park Ct. NP20 10 D4
Stelvio Park Cres. NP20 10 D4
Stelvio Park Dri. NP20 10 D4
*Stephen Walk, Cefn Wood. NP10 4 D4
Stephenson St. NP19 14 C1
Sterndale Bennett Rd. NP19 13 G2
Stevenson Clo. NP10 4 C2
Stevenson Ct. NP10 4 C2
Stockton Clo. NP19 7 H4
Stockton Rd. NP19 7 H5
Stockwood Clo. NP18 17 B2
Stockwood Vw. NP18 17 B2
Stow Hill. NP20 5 A5
Stow Park Av. NP20 5 A5
Stow Park Circle. NP20 10 D4
Stow Park Cres. NP20 5 A5
Stow Park Dri. NP20 5 A6
Stow Park Gdns. NP20 10 D4
Straits La. NP18 15 H5
Sullivan Circle. NP19 13 F3
Summerhill Av. NP19 12 A1
*Summerhill Ho, Albert Av. NP19 12 A2
Sunningdale Ct. NP19 13 E1
Sunnybank. NP10 4 B6
Surrey Pl. NP19 8 A6
Sussex Clo. NP19 12 C5
Sutherland Cres. NP19 8 C6
Sutton Rd. NP19 7 H5
Swallow Way. NP10 16 C2
Sward Clo. NP10 4 C1
Sycamore Av. NP19 12 C3
Sylvan Clo. NP20 7 F2

Talbot La. NP20 5 C4
Taliesin Clo. NP10 4 D2
Taliesin Dri. NP10 4 D2
Tallis Clo. NP19 13 G2
Tamar Clo. NP20 6 C3
Tanhouse Dri. NP18 9 E3
Tees Clo. NP20 6 D3
Telford Clo. NP10 4 D2
Telford St. NP19 12 A3
Temple St. NP20 11 G5
Tenby Clo. NP10 16 C4
Tennyson Rd. NP19 12 B2
Tetbury Clo. NP20 7 F6
Tewkesbury Walk. NP20 5 C1
Thames Clo. NP20 6 C3
The Brades. NP18 8 D1
The Bryn. NP20 6 C2
The Cedars. NP18 17 E4
The Coppins. NP20 7 E2
The Courtyard. NP10 16 B3
The Firs. NP20 7 F3
The Glen. NP18 17 C2
The Griffin. NP10 4 C6
The Hawthorns. NP18 8 D2
The Mews. NP20 10 D2
The Moorings. NP19 8 A4
The Nurseries. NP18 17 C2
The Paddocks. NP18 8 A1
The Redlands. NP19 13 E3
The Rosegarden. NP20 10 D2
The Spinney. NP20 7 F3
The Turnstiles. NP20 7 G5
The Uplands. NP10 4 B2
Third St. NP19 15 E2
Thirlmere Pl. NP19 8 A5
Thomas Gro. NP10 4 D4
Thompson Av. NP19 12 D4
Thompson Clo. NP19 12 D4
Thornbury Park. NP10 4 C4
Thornhill Gdns. NP10 4 A1
Thornhill Way. NP10 4 A1
Till Gro. NP18 8 A2
Tippet Clo. NP19 13 G2
Tom Mann Clo. NP19 9 F6
Tone Clo. NP20 6 B3
Tone Rd. NP20 6 B3
Tone Sq. NP20 6 B2
Toronto Clo. NP20 10 B4
Torridge Rd. NP20 6 A2
Tram Rd. NP18 8 D2
Traston Av. NP19 12 D6
Traston Clo. NP19 12 D6
Traston La. NP19 12 D6
Traston Rd. NP19 12 D6
Traws Mawr Rd. NP20 6 B2
Treberth Estate. NP19 13 F1
Tredegar Ct. NP20 11 G5
Tredegar House Dri. NP10 16 C3
Tredegar Park View. NP10 10 A3
Tredegar St, Newport. NP20 5 D6
Tredegar St, Rhiwderin. NP10 4 A5
Tregare St. NP19 5 D2
Tregarn Clo. NP18 17 E1
Tregarn Ct. NP18 17 E1
Tregarn Rd. NP18 17 D1
Tregwilym Clo. NP10 4 C4
Tregwilym Rd. NP10 4 B3
Trent Rd. NP20 6 B2
Trevithick Clo. NP20 6 D1
Trinity Ct. NP20 11 G5
Trinity La. NP18 8 B2
Trinity Pl. NP20 11 G5
Trinity View. NP18 8 A2
Trostrey St. NP19 11 G1
Tudor Cres. NP10 4 D4
Tudor Rd. NP19 8 A5
Tulip Wk. NP10 4 A2
Tunnel Ter. NP20 5 A4
Turner St. NP19 11 G1
Tweedy La. NP19 12 B2
Ty-Coch Clo. NP10 4 B6
Tydu View. NP10 4 D3
Tyllwyd Rd. NP20 10 D3
Tyne Clo. NP20 6 B4
Union St. NP20 11 H5
Uplands Ct. NP10 12 B1
Upper Dock St. NP20 5 C3
Upper Tennyson Rd. NP19 12 B2
Upton La. NP20 10 D3
Upton Rd. NP20 10 D3
Usk Rd. NP18 8 D2
Usk St. NP19 7 H6
Usk Vale Clo. NP18 8 D2
Usk Vale Dri. NP18 8 D2
Usk Vale Mews. NP18 8 D2
Uskway. NP20 5 D4

Vale View. NP19 8 C6
Van Dyke Clo. NP19 8 B5
Vanbrugh Clo. NP10 4 D2
Vancouver Dri. NP20 10 B4
Vaughan Williams Dri. NP19 13 E2
Vermeer Cres. NP19 8 C6
Veronica Clo. NP10 4 D5
Vicarage Clo. NP10 4 D6
Vicarage Gdns. NP10 4 B2
Vicarage Hill. NP20 5 B5
Victoria Av. NP19 12 A2
Victoria Clo. NP20 5 C5
Victoria Ct. NP19 12 A2
Victoria Cres. NP20 5 B4
Victoria Pl. NP20 5 C4
Victoria Rd. NP20 5 C5
Victoria Walk. NP20 5 C5
*Vine Cotts, Norman St. NP18 8 D3
Vine Pl. NP19 11 H1
Viscount Evan Dri. NP10 16 D2
Vivian Rd. NP19 12 A3

Walden Grange Clo. NP19 12 D2
Walford Davies Dri. NP19 13 E2
Walford St. NP20 7 F5
Wallis St. NP20 11 H5
Walmer Rd. NP19 12 B2
Walnut Dri. NP18 8 A3
Walsall St. NP19 12 A3
Walton Clo. NP19 13 E3
Waltwood Park Dri. NP18 17 F4
Waltwood Rd. NP18 17 D4
Ward Clo. NP19 8 C6
Warlock Clo. NP19 13 G2
*Warwick La, Warwick Rd. NP19 12 C2
Warwick Rd. NP19 12 C2
Watch House Par. NP20 11 G6
Waterloo Rd. NP20 11 E4
Waters La. NP20 5 C4
Waterside Clo. NP10 4 C1
*Watkins La, Ombersley La. NP20 10 D3
*Watson Walk, Cefn Wood. NP10 4 D4
Watt Clo. NP20 7 E2
Watts Clo. NP10 4 D2
Wavell Dri. NP20 7 E1
Waveney Clo. NP20 6 A2
Weare Clo. NP20 6 A2
Wednesbury St. NP19 12 B3
Welland Circle. NP20 6 A3
Welland Cres. NP20 6 A3
Wellington Rd. NP20 10 B4
Wells Clo. NP20 10 C6
Wentwood Rd. NP18 8 A3
Wentworth Clo. NP10 4 B5
Wern Ter. NP10 4 B2
Wesley Pl. NP20 5 C4
West Market St. NP20 5 D6
West Nash Rd. NP18 15 G6
West Park Rd. NP20 10 D3
West St. NP20 5 B4
Western Av. NP20 10 A3
Western Valley Rd. NP10 4 D4
Westfield Av. NP20 7 E3
Westfield Clo. NP18 8 A1
Westfield Dri. NP20 7 E3
Westfield Rd. NP18 8 A1
Westfield Rd. NP20 10 D2
Westfield Way. NP20 7 E3
Westgate Ct. NP18 8 C3
Westmoor Clo. NP19 13 E4
Westray Clo. NP19 8 B6
Westville Rd. NP20 10 D3
Westway Rd. NP20 14 A1
Wharf La. NP19 11 H2
Wharf Rd. NP19 11 H2
Wheeler St. NP20 5 C1
Whistler Clo. NP19 8 B5
Whitby Pl. NP19 11 G1
White Av. NP10 16 C4
White Hart La. NP18 8 D3
Whiteash Glade. NP18 8 A3
Whitstone Rd. NP19 12 D1
Whittle Ct. NP20 7 E1
Whittle Dri. NP20 6 D1
Willenhall St. NP19 11 H3
William Lovett Gdns. NP20 5 A4
William Morris Dri. NP19 9 F6
*Williams Clo, Capel Clo. 20 11 G4
Willow Clo. NP10 4 A1
Willow Clo. NP19 12 D5
Willow Grn. NP18 8 A1
Willow Ter. NP18 17 E4
Wills Row. NP10 4 D4
Wilson Rd. NP19 8 C6
Wilson St. NP20 11 H5
Winchester Clo. NP20 10 D6
Windermere Sq. NP19 8 A4
*Windmill Sq, Mountjoy St. NP20 5 C3
Windrush Clo. NP20 6 C3
Windsor Pl. NP10 4 D4
Windsor Rd. NP19 12 B2
Windsor Ter. NP20 5 A4
Wingate St. NP20 11 G6
Winmill St. NP20 11 G4
Wistaria Clo. NP20 7 E1
Witham St. NP19 11 H3
*Wolseley Clo, Wolseley St. NP20 11 G6
Wolseley St. NP20 11 G6
*Wolseley St Clo, Wolseley St. NP20 11 G6
Wood Clo. NP10 4 C1
Wood Cres. NP10 4 C1
Woodland Dri, Bassaleg. NP10 4 B5
Woodland Dri, Rogerstone. NP10 4 A1
Woodland Park Rd. NP19 12 B1

Woodland Rd, Llanmartin. NP18 17 E4
Woodland Rd, Newport. NP19 12 B1
Woodlands Dri. NP26 7 E1
Woodside. NP10 16 C2
Woodville Rd. NP20 10 C3
Worcester Cres. NP19 8 B5
Wordsworth Rd. NP19 12 B2
Wrenford Ct. NP20 5 C5
Wright Clo. NP19 12 C4
Wye Cres. NP20 6 C3
Wyvenre Rd. NP19 12 C2
Wyndham St. NP20 5 C1

Yeo Clo. NP20 6 B3
Yeo Rd. NP20 6 C3
Yewberry Clo. NP20 7 F3
Yewberry La. NP20 7 F3
Yewtree La. NP18 8 D2
York Pl. NP20 5 A4
York Rd. NP19 7 H6

CALDICOT

Alianore Rd. NP26 19 B4
Angiddy Clo. NP26 19 C2
Arthurs Ct. NP26 19 E3
Ash Gro. NP26 19 B2
Avon Clo. NP26 19 B2
Beech Rd. NP26 19 A2
Betjeman Av. NP26 19 A4
Birbeck Rd. NP26 19 A3
Blackbird Rd. NP26 19 C4
Budden Cres. NP26 19 B2
Burns Cres. NP26 19 A3
Byron Pl. NP26 19 A4
Cae Mawr Av. NP26 19 B3
Cae Mawr Gro. NP26 19 B3
Cae Mawr Rd. NP26 19 B3
Caldicot By-Pass. NP26 19 B4
Caldicot Rd. NP26 19 E3
Canterbury Way. NP26 19 F3
Cas Troggy. NP26 19 B2
Castle Gdns. NP26 19 B2
Castle Lea. NP26 19 C3
Castle Lodge Clo. NP26 19 D3
Castle Lodge Cres. NP26 19 D3
Castle Lodge Dri. NP26 19 D3
Castle Way. NP26 19 D3
Chaucer Clo. NP26 19 A4
Chepstow Rd. NP26 19 C3
Church Clo. NP26 19 C2
Church Rd. NP26 19 C2
Churchfield Av. NP26 19 B2
Cil-y-Coed Way. NP26 19 C1
Clos Aled. NP26 19 C2
Clos Alwen. NP26 19 C1
Clos Glaslyn. NP26 19 C1
Clos Rheidol. NP26 19 C1
Cobb Cres. NP26 19 B4
Crick Rd. NP26 19 F3
Curlew Av. NP26 19 C4
Cwrt Severn. NP26 19 A4
Dangarga Dri. NP26 19 B3
Deepweir. NP26 19 D3
Deepwier Gdns. NP26 19 D4
Denny View. NP26 19 D4
Dewstow Clo. NP26 19 A3
Dewstow Gdns. NP26 19 A3
Dewstow Rd. NP26 19 A2
Dunlin Av. NP26 19 B4
Durand Rd. NP26 19 B4
Eagle Clo. NP26 19 C4
Ebbw Rd. NP26 19 B2
Elan Way. NP26 19 C2
Elm Rd. NP26 19 B2
Estuary View. NP26 19 D4
Fairfield Clo. NP26 19 C4
Falcon Clo. NP26 19 C4
Fernleigh Rd. NP26 19 A3
Firs Rd. NP26 19 A2
Fitzwalter Rd. NP26 19 B4
Garthalan Dri. NP26 19 A4
Goldfinch Clo. NP26 19 B4
Green Av. NP26 19 B3
Green La. NP26 19 B3
Greenfield. NP26 19 B3
Grey Hill View. NP26 19 E3
Grove Gdns. NP26 19 B2
Hazel Av. NP26 19 A2
Herbert Rd. NP26 19 B2
Heol Towy. NP26 19 C1

Heron Rd. NP26 19 C4
Honddu Clo. NP26 19 B2
INDUSTRIAL & RETAIL:
Pill Farm
  Trading Est. NP26 19 E4
Severn Bridge
  Ind Est. NP26 19 E3
Jolyons Ct. NP26 19 C3
Jubilee Way. NP26 19 B3
Keats Rd. NP26 19 A3
Kestrel Clo. NP26 19 C4
Kingfisher Clo. NP26 19 C4
Kipling Rd. NP26 19 A3
Kirrlach Clo. NP26 19 A3
Lapwing Av. NP26 19 C4
Linnet Rd. NP26 19 B4
Llanthony Clo. NP26 19 C2
Lodge Way. NP26 19 E3
Longcroft Rd. NP26 19 B3
Longfellow Clo. NP26 19 A3
Longfellow Ct. NP26 19 A4
Longfellow Rd. NP26 19 A3
Main Rd. NP26 19 F3
Mallard Av. NP26 19 B4
Manor Way. NP26 19 F3
Maple Clo. NP26 19 B2
Margretts Way. NP26 19 B2
Masefield Rd. NP26 19 A4
Mill La. NP26 19 B3
Millfield La. NP26 19 C3
Monks Clo. NP26 19 C2
Moorlands View. NP26 19 D4
Mount Ballan. NP26 19 D1
Neddern Ct. NP26 19 B2
Neddern Way. NP26 19 B2
New Rd. NP26 19 A3
Newport Rd. NP26 19 A3
Nightingale Clo. NP26 19 C4
Norman Ct. NP26 19 B3
Norman Way. NP26 19 E4
Oaklands Park. NP26 19 F3
Oakley Clo. NP26 19 A2
Oakley Way. NP26 19 A2
Orchard Clo. NP26 19 B3
Orchard Gdns. NP26 19 E3
Orchid Dri. NP26 19 D4
Osprey Dri. NP26 19 C4
Park Rd. NP26 19 A2
Pill Row. NP26 19 D3
Pill Way. NP26 19 E3
Plover Cres. NP26 19 C4
Plum Tree La. NP26 19 B4
Priory Clo. NP26 19 B2
Prospect Cres. NP26 19 A4
Railway View. NP26 19 D4
Rogiet Rd. NP26 19 A3
St Marys Pl. NP26 19 F3
Sandy La. NP26 19 B2
Severn View. NP26 19 A3
Shakespeare Clo. NP26 19 A3
Shakespeare Dri. NP26 19 A3
*Shakespeare Row,
  Shakespeare Dri. NP26 19 A3
Shelley Clo. NP26 19 A3
Southbrook Vw. NP26 19 E4
Stafford Rd. NP26 19 B4
Station Rd. NP26 19 A4
Statton Clo. NP26 19 A4
Sudbrook Rd. NP26 19 F3
Swallow Clo. NP26 19 C4
Swallow Dri. NP26 19 C4
Sycamore Av. NP26 19 A2
Symondscliff Way. NP26 19 E4
Taff Rd. NP26 19 C2
Tennyson Clo. NP26 19 A3
Tennyson Rd. NP26 19 A3
The Avenue. NP26 19 A4
The Close, Caldicot. NP26 19 A3
The Close, Portskewett. NP26 19 F3
The Cross. NP26 19 C3
Treetops. NP26 19 E3
Tronddi Clo. NP26 19 B2
Usk Clo. NP26 19 C2
Waghausel Clo. NP26 19 B3
Wentwood View. NP26 19 B3
*West End Shopping Centre,
  Newport Rd. NP26 19 A3
Westfield. NP26 19 A3
Westfield Av. NP26 19 A3
Wiesental Clo. NP26 19 C2
Willow Clo. NP26 19 B2
Woodland Clo. NP26 19 B2

Woodstock Clo. NP26 19 B3
Woodstock Ct. NP26 19 B4
Woodstock Way. NP26 19 B4
Wordsworth Clo. NP26 19 A4
Yewtree Clo. NP26 19 B3

CHEPSTOW

*Albion Sq,
  Thomas St. NP16 20 C3
Alexandra Rd. NP16 21 C5
Alice Cres. NP16 21 D7
Alma Dri. NP16 21 D6
Alpha Rd. NP16 21 C5
Apprentice Clo. NP16 21 F6
Arlington Ct. NP16 20 E3
Ash Clo. NP16 21 B5
Aust Cres. NP16 21 C6
Badgers Dene. NP16 20 B3
Bank St. NP16 20 C3
Barnets Wood. NP16 20 A3
Beachley Rd. NP16 20 D1
*Beaufort Sq,
  High St. NP16 20 C3
Beech Gro. NP16 20 B4
Bigstone Clo. NP16 20 D1
Bigstone Gro. NP16 20 D1
Bishops Clo. NP16 21 D6
Bluebell Dri. NP16 21 D5
Bridge St. NP16 20 C2
Bridget Dri. NP16 20 E4
Briton Clo. NP16 21 D6
Brunel Rd. NP16 21 B5
Bulwark Av. NP16 21 C5
Bulwark Rd. NP16 20 B3
Burnt Barn Rd. NP16 21 C6
Buttington Rd. NP16 20 E3
Buttington Ter. NP16 20 F4
Caerwent La. NP16 21 D7
Caird St. NP16 20 C3
Castle Gdns. NP16 20 B2
Castle View. NP16 20 D2
Castle Wood. NP16 20 A3
Castleford Gdns. NP16 20 C1
Castleford Hill. NP16 20 C1
Cedar Clo. NP16 21 B5
Celandine Ct. NP16 21 D5
Channel View. NP16 21 B5
Chartist Way. NP16 21 C6
Church Rd. NP16 20 C2
Church Row. NP16 20 C2
Cider Mill Clo. NP16 21 D6
Clarendon Clo. NP16 21 D6
Cliff View. NP16 20 E4
Coleford Rd. NP16 20 D1
Collingwood Clo. NP16 21 D6
Conwy Dri. NP16 21 C7
Cromwell Rd. NP16 21 C5
Danes Clo. NP16 20 B3
*Davis Ct,
  Bridge St. NP16 20 C2
Deans Gdns. NP16 20 A2
Deans Hill. NP16 20 B3
Dell View. NP16 20 C3
Denbigh Dri. NP16 21 D6
Denmark Dri. NP16 20 E4
Edmond Rd. NP16 20 E2
Elm Clo. NP16 20 E1
Elm Rd. NP16 20 D1
Elmdale. NP16 20 C2
Exmouth Pl. NP16 20 C3
Fair View. NP16 20 B4
Fairfield Rd. NP16 20 C4
Fedw Wood. NP16 20 A2
Fern Clo. NP16 21 D6
Ferry Way. NP16 21 F6
Fishermans Walk. NP16 21 D6
Fitzosborn Clo. NP16 20 B3
Fountain Way. NP16 21 D7
Garden City Way. NP16 20 C3
Garvey Clo. NP16 21 D6
Gibraltar Way. NP16 21 F6
Gloucester Rd. NP16 20 D1
Grahamstown Gro. NP16 20 E2
Grahamstown Rd. NP16 20 E3
Grasmere Way. NP16 21 E6
Green St. NP16 20 C3
Gwentlands Clo. NP16 20 B4
Gwy Ct. NP16 20 C2
Hanover Ct, Chepstow. NP16 20 B3
Hanover Ct, Sedbury. NP16 20 E3

Hardwick Av. NP16 20 C3
Hardwick Hill. NP16 20 B3
Hardwick Hill La. NP16 20 B3
Hardwick Ter. NP16 20 B3
Hawthorn Clo. NP16 21 C6
Heather Clo. NP16 21 D5
Hendrick Dri. NP16 20 E3
High Beech La. NP16 20 A4
High St. NP16 20 C3
High View. NP16 20 B3
Hilltop. NP16 20 B4
Hitchen Hollow. NP16 21 F7
Hocker Hill St. NP16 20 C2
Hollins Clo. NP16 20 C2
Holly Clo. NP16 21 C6
Hopewell Clo. NP16 21 E6
Howells Row. NP16 20 C2
Hughes Cres. NP16 20 C4
Huntfield Rd. NP16 20 A2
INDUSTRIAL & RETAIL:
Newhouse Farm
  Ind Est. NP16 21 C8
Sedbury Business Pk.
  NP16 20 F2
Inner Loop Rd. NP16 21 F5
Kendall Sq. NP16 20 D2
King Alfreds Rd. NP16 20 E4
Kingsmark La. NP16 20 A2
Laburnum Way. NP16 21 B5
Lady Margaret Ct. NP16 21 D6
Lancaster Way. NP16 20 B2
*Langham Ho,
  Thornwell Rd. NP16 21 C5
Larkfield Av. NP16 20 B4
Larkfield Pk. NP16 20 B5
Larkhill Clo. NP16 20 B4
Lewis Way. NP16 21 D6
*Library Pl,
  Bank St. NP16 20 C3
Linden Clo. NP16 20 B4
Loop Rd. NP16 21 F5
Lord Eldon Dri. NP16 20 C4
Lower Church St. NP16 20 C2
Madocke Rd. NP16 20 E3
Magnolia Clo. NP16 21 D6
*Manor Way,
  Bank St. NP16 20 C3
Maple Av. NP16 21 B5
Mariners Reach. NP16 21 E6
Marsh Rd. NP16 21 C5
Marten Rd. NP16 20 C4
Mathern Rd. NP16 20 B4
Mathern Way. NP16 21 C5
Meadow Wk. NP16 20 B3
Meads Clo. NP16 21 C5
Mercian Way. NP16 20 E4
Middle St. NP16 20 C2
Middle Way. NP16 21 D5
Mill La. NP16 20 C3
*Montague Almshouse,
  Upper Church St. NP16 20 C2
Moor St. NP16 20 C3
Mopla Rd. NP16 20 C1
Mount Pleasant. NP16 20 B3
Mount Way. NP16 20 B2
Mounton Clo. NP16 20 B3
Mounton Dri. NP16 20 B3
Mounton Rd. NP16 20 A3
Myrtle Pl. NP16 20 D2
Nelson St. NP16 20 C3
Newport Rd. NP16 20 B4
Normandy Way. NP16 20 A2
Norse Way. NP16 20 E3
Oak Clo. NP16 21 B6
Oakfield Av. NP16 20 A2
Offas Clo. NP16 20 E4
Old Bulwark Rd. NP16 20 C4
Old Oak Clo. NP16 21 B6
Orchard Av. NP16 21 B5
Orchard Farm Clo. NP16 20 E4
Orchard Gdns. NP16 20 C2
Ormerod Rd. NP16 20 E3
Park View, Chepstow. NP16 20 A2
Park View, Sedbury. NP16 20 E3
Pembroke Rd. NP16 21 C5
Penda Pl. NP16 20 E3
Penterry Pk. NP16 20 A3
Phoenix Dri. NP16 21 D6
Piercefield Av. NP16 20 C4
Port Wall. NP16 20 C3
Portwall Rd. NP16 20 C3
Potters Croft. NP16 21 F6

Preston Clo. NP16 2?
Priory Clo. NP16 2?
Queens Rd. NP16 2?
Raglan Way. NP16 2?
Redwood Clo. NP16 2?
Regent Way. NP16 2?
Restway Wall. NP16 2?
*Riflemans Way,
  Bank St. NP16 20
River Vw. NP16 20
Rock Villa La. NP16 20
Rockwood Rd. NP16 20
Rougemont Gro. NP16 2?
Rowan Dri. NP16 2?
Ruffetts Clo. NP16 20
St Andrews Av. NP16 20
St Anns St. NP16 20
St Davids Clo. NP16 20
St Ewens Rd. NP16 2?
St George Rd. NP16 20
St Georges Way. NP16 2?
St Johns Gdns. NP16 20
St Kingsmark Av. NP16 20
St Lawrence La. NP16 20
St Lawrence Pk. NP16 20
St Lawrence Rd. NP16 20
St Marys St. NP16 20
St Maur Gdns. NP16 20
St Tecla Rd. NP16 20
St Tewdric Rd. NP16 20
Saxon Pl. NP16 20
School Hill. NP16 20
Sedbury La. NP16 20
Severn Av. NP16 20
Severn Cres. NP16 20
Sharps Way. NP16 21
Silleys Clo. NP16 20
Somerset Way. NP16 21
Station Rd. NP16 20
Steep St. NP16 20
Striguil Rd. NP16 21
Strongbow Rd. NP16 20
Stuart Clo. NP18 20
Summer House La. 20
Sycamore Av. NP16 21
Tallards Pl. NP16 20
Tempest Clo. NP16 20
Tempest Way. NP16 20
Tenby La. NP16 21
The Back. NP16 21
The Headland. NP16 20
The Hop Gdn. NP16 21
The Martins. NP16 20
The Myrtles. NP16 20
The Octagon. NP16 21
The Old Hill. NP16 20
The Paddock. NP16 20
The Priory. NP16 20
The Reddings. NP16 21
The Yetts. NP16 20
*Thomas Powis Almshouse,
  Bridge St. NP16 20
Thomas St. NP16 20
Thorn Tree Dri. NP16 21
Thornwell Rd. NP16 20
Tudor Dri. NP16 20
Turnpike Rd. NP16 20
Turnpike End. NP16 21
Tutshill Gdns. NP16 20
Tylers Way. NP16 20
Upper Church St. NP16 20
Upper Nelson St. NP16 20
Valentine La. NP16 21
Vauxhall La. NP16 20
Vauxhall Rd. NP16 20
Victoria Rd. NP16 21
Wallwern Wood. NP16 20
Warren Slade. NP16 20
Warwick Clo. NP16 20
Waters Rd. NP16 20
Well Clo. NP16 21
Welsh St. NP16 20
Western Av. NP16 21
Willow Clo. NP16 21
Wintour Clo. NP16 20
Wirewood Clo. NP16 20
Wirewood Cres. NP16 20
Wye Cres. NP16 20
Wye Valley Link Rd. NP16 20
Wyebank Av. NP16 20
Wyebank Clo. NP16 20
Wyebank Cres. NP16 20
Wyebank Pl. NP16 20
Wyebank Rise. NP16 20

MAGOR

bank Rd. NP16	20 D3
bank View. NP16	20 E3
bank Way. NP16	20 D3
ia Av. NP26	18 D2
le Av. NP26	18 E2
gton Clo. NP26	18 E3
gers Walk. NP26	18 E2
land St. NP26	18 A4
ns Ct. NP26	18 E3
n Clo. NP26	18 D2
k Hall. NP26	18 C3
heim Av. NP26	18 B2
heim Clo. NP26	18 B3
heim Ct. NP26	18 C2
heim Dri. NP26	18 C2
heim Gdns. NP26	18 B2
heim Park. NP26	18 C2
ssknockers St. NP26	18 C3
r Clo. NP26	18 D2
ewell Gdns. NP26	18 F3
adlands Clo. NP26	18 E3
ic Clo. NP26	18 E3
pel Ter. NP26	18 D2
stnut Clo. NP26	18 C3
rch Rd. NP26	18 F3
ssways Clo. NP26	18 F3
vleaze. NP26	18 C2
cing Clo. NP26	18 D2
cing Hill. NP26	18 D2
ch Hill. NP26	18 D2
a Av. NP26	18 E3
as Hill. NP26	18 E3
nge Rd. NP26	18 D2
en Moor La. NP26	18 B3
yndy Rd. NP26	18 E2
vthorn Clo. NP26	18 D2
onston Clo. NP26	18 E3
nters Ridge. NP26	18 E3
nsington Pk. NP26	18 B3
n Way. NP26	18 E2
urnum Clo. NP26	18 D2
dau Clo. NP26	18 D2
ngley Clo. NP26	18 C2
urel Clo. NP26	18 E2
urel Cres. NP26	18 E3
a Clo. NP26	18 D2
nwern Rd. NP26	18 A4
gor Rd. NP26	18 A1
in Rd. NP26	18 D3
nor Chase. NP26	18 E3
eadow Rise. NP26	18 D2
ll Common. NP26	18 D3

Mill Reen. NP26	18 D2
Millbrook Ct. NP26	18 D3
Millfield Park. NP26	18 D2
Miskin Ct. NP26	18 F3
Netherwent View. NP26	18 C2
Newport Rd. NP26	18 B2
Oak Clo. NP26	18 D2
Old Barn Ct. NP26	18 F2
Old Stone Rd. NP26	18 E2
Park Ct. NP26	18 F3
Pembroke Clo. NP26	18 F2
Pembroke Ct. NP26	18 F2
Penegrine Ct. NP26	18 E2
Pennyfarthing La. NP26	18 D3
Priory Ct. NP26	18 C3
Quarry Rise. NP26	18 D2
Queens Gdns. NP26	18 C2
Rectory Gdns. NP26	18 E3
Rockfield Cres. NP26	18 E2
Rockfield Gro. NP26	18 F2
Rockfield Rise. NP26	18 E2
Rockfield Vw. NP26	18 E2
Rockfield Way. NP26	18 E2
Rowan Clo. NP26	18 E2
St Annes Cres. NP26	18 F3
St Brides Clo. NP26	18 C2
St Brides Rd. NP26	18 C1
St Dubricius Gdns. NP26	18 F3
St Marys Croft. NP26	18 F3
St Mellons Clo. NP26	18 E2
St Stephens Clo. NP26	18 F3
St Stephens Pl. NP26	18 F2
*Sycamore Ter, Brassknockers St. NP26	18 C3
Teal Clo. NP26	18 E2
The Briars. NP26	18 C3
The Gardens. NP26	18 C2
The Greenways. NP26	18 C3
The Lawns. NP26	18 C3
The Limes. NP26	18 D2
The Meadow. NP26	18 C3
The Paddocks. NP26	18 F2
The Plantation. NP26	18 D3
The Ramp. NP26	18 E3
The Square. NP26	18 C3
The Willows. NP26	18 D3
Tredegar Dri. NP26	18 E2
Tudor Ct. NP26	18 E3
Tump La. NP26	18 E3
Victoria Way. NP26	18 D3
Vinegar Hill. NP26	18 D1
West End. NP26	18 C3
West End Gdns. NP16	18 E3
*Wheatsheaf Ct, Newport Rd. NP26	18 B2

Whitechapel Wk. NP26	18 E2
Whitehall Gdns. NP26	18 E3
Whitewall. NP26	18 D3
Windsor Clo. NP26	18 C3
Windsor Dri. NP26	18 C3
Windsor Gdns. NP26	18 C3
Windsor Pk. NP26	18 C3
Withy Clo. NP26	18 C3
Withy Walk. NP26	18 C3
Woodbine Gdns. NP26	18 D3
Yew Tree Clo. NP26	18 E3

RISCA

Almond Av. NP11	3 D2
Arran Clo. NP11	3 E3
Aster Clo. NP11	3 D2
Azalea Rd. NP11	3 E4
*Belvedere Ter, Temperance Hill. NP11	3 B1
Birch Grove. NP11	3 C2
Bluebell Way. NP11	3 F4
Bredon Clo. NP11	3 E3
Bridge St. NP11	3 B2
Brierley Clo. NP11	3 E3
Brookland Rd. NP11	3 C3
*Buttercup Clo, Bluebell Way. NP11	3 F4
Caderidris Clo. NP11	3 E2
Camellia Av. NP11	3 F4
Campanula Dri. NP11	3 F4
Channel View. NP11	3 D3
Chartist Ct. NP11	3 D3
Cheviot Clo. NP11	3 E2
Chiltern Clo. NP11	3 F3
Church Rd. NP11	3 B1
Clarence Pl. NP11	3 B2
Cleveland Dri. NP11	3 E3
Clifton St. NP11	3 F4
Clyde St. NP11	3 C3
Commercial St. NP11	3 C3
Coronation St. NP11	3 C3
Cotswold Way. NP11	3 E2
Crescent Rd. NP11	3 A1
Cromwell Rd. NP11	3 A1
Cwrt yr Ysgol. NP11	3 B1
Daffodil La. NP11	3 F4
Dan-y-graig. NP11	3 A1
Dan-y-graig Rd. NP11	3 B2
Darran Rd. NP11	3 A1
Delphinium Rd. NP11	3 F4
Dewberry Gro. NP11	3 F4
Ebbw St. NP11	3 B2
Elm Dri. NP11	3 D2

Eppynt Clo. NP11	3 E2
Exchange Rd. NP11	3 B1
Fairview Av. NP11	3 C2
Fernlea. NP11	3 B1
Fields Rd. NP11	3 D4
Forsythia Clo. NP11	3 E3
Francis St. NP11	3 D3
Gelli Av. NP11	3 C2
Gelli Clo. NP11	3 C2
Gelli Cres. NP11	3 C2
*Gerbera Dri., Camellia Av NP11	3 F4
Graig View. NP11	3 B2
Grove Rd. NP11	3 B1
Gwendoline Rd. NP11	3 B2
Herbert Av. NP11	3 D3
Highfield Clo. NP11	3 B2
Hill St. NP11	3 C2
Holly Rd. NP11	3 C2
INDUSTRIAL & RETAIL:	
Pontymister Ind Est. NP11	3 C4
Islwyn Clo. NP11	3 D3
Islwyn Ct. NP11	3 D3
Jasmine Clo. NP11	3 F4
Leydene Clo. NP11	3 B1
Lilac Gro. NP11	3 F4
Llanarth Sq. NP11	3 C3
Lower Wyndham Ter. NP11	3 D3
Lyne Rd. NP11	3 C3
Machen Clo. NP11	3 D3
Machen St. NP11	3 B2
Malvern Clo. NP11	3 F3
Malvern Ter. NP11	3 C3
Manor Rd. NP11	3 D3
Manor Way. NP11	3 D3
Maple Av. NP11	3 D2
Maple Gdns. NP11	3 E4
Maryland Rd. NP11	3 C3
Meadow Cres. NP11	3 E4
Meadowland Dri. NP11	3 F4
Mendip Clo. NP11	3 F3
Mill St. NP11	3 D3
Mill Ter. NP11	3 D3
Moriah Hill. NP11	3 C2
Mount Pleasant Rd. NP11	3 C2
Mount Rd. NP11	3 C2
Mountain Rd. NP11	3 E1
Mountside. NP11	3 F3
Navigation Rd. NP11	3 B1
New Park Rd. NP11	3 A1
Newport Rd. NP11	3 D4
Park Pl. NP11	3 C3
Park Rd. NP11	3 B2
Pennine Clo. NP11	3 F2

Penrhiw Rd. NP11	3 C2
Pentland Clo. NP11	3 F3
*Petunia Wk, Gerbera Dri. NP11	3 E4
Phillip St. NP11	3 B2
Pine Clo. NP11	3 C2
Pontymason La. NP11	3 F3
Preseli Clo. NP11	3 E2
Primrose Way. NP11	3 F4
Priory St. NP11	3 C2
Quantock Clo. NP11	3 E2
Raglan St. NP11	3 A1
Railway St. NP11	3 B1
Ravenswood Ct. NP11	3 A1
Rifleman St. NP11	3 B1
Risca Rd. NP11	3 F4
Rivermead Way. NP11	3 F4
Rosemont Av. NP11	3 C2
Rowan Rd. NP11	3 D2
St Mary St. NP11	3 B1
Sansom St. NP11	3 B1
Sarn Pl. NP11	3 B1
Severn Clo. NP11	3 D3
Snowdon Clo. NP11	3 D2
Snowdrop La. NP11	3 F4
Springfield Rd. NP11	3 D3
Station Rd. NP11	3 C3
Sycamore Cres. NP11	3 D3
Tanybryn. NP11	3 E4
Taylor St. NP11	3 B1
Temperance Hill. NP11	3 B1
Thistle Way. NP11	3 F4
Tir-y-Cwm Rd. NP11	3 B2
Tir-y-Cwm La. NP11	3 B2
Trafalgar St. NP11	3 C3
Tredegar St. NP11	3 B2
Tredegar Ter. NP11	3 B3
Trinity St. NP11	3 B2
Twmbarlwm Clo. NP11	3 E2
Ty-Isaf Cres. NP11	3 D4
Ty-Isaf Park Av. NP11	3 E4
Ty-Isaf Park Circle. NP11	3 D4
Ty-Isaf Park Rd. NP11	3 E4
Ty-Isaf Park Villas. NP11	3 D4
Tyn-y-Cwm Rd. NP11	3 E4
Vale View. NP11	3 C2
Well Spring Ter. NP11	3 C3
Wentwood Pl. NP11	3 E3
Wesley Pl. NP11	3 B2
Wood View Cres. NP11	3 C2
Wood View Rd. NP11	3 C2
Wyndham Ter. NP11	3 D2
York Pl. NP11	3 B1

ESTATE PUBLICATIONS

RED BOOKS

ALDERSHOT, CAMBERLEY
ALFRETON, BELPER, RIPLEY
ASHFORD, TENTERDEN
AYLESBURY, TRING
BANGOR, CAERNARFON
BARNSTAPLE, ILFRACOMBE
BASILDON, BILLERICAY
BASINGSTOKE, ANDOVER
BATH, BRADFORD-ON-AVON
BEDFORD
BIRMINGHAM, WOLVERHAMPTON, COVENTRY
BODMIN, WADEBRIDGE
BOURNEMOUTH, POOLE, CHRISTCHURCH
BRACKNELL
BRENTWOOD
BRIGHTON, LEWES, NEWHAVEN, SEAFORD
BRISTOL
BROMLEY (London Bromley)
BURTON-UPON-TRENT, SWADLINCOTE
BURY ST. EDMUNDS
CAMBRIDGE
CARDIFF
CARLISLE
CHELMSFORD, BRAINTREE, MALDON, WITHAM
CHESTER
CHESTERFIELD
CHICHESTER, BOGNOR REGIS
COLCHESTER, CLACTON
CORBY, KETTERING
COVENTRY
CRAWLEY & MID SUSSEX
CREWE
DERBY, HEANOR, CASTLE DONINGTON
EASTBOURNE, BEXHILL, SEAFORD, NEWHAVEN
EDINBURGH, MUSSELBURGH, PENICUIK
EXETER, EXMOUTH
FALKIRK, GRANGEMOUTH
FAREHAM, GOSPORT
FLINTSHIRE TOWNS
FOLKESTONE, DOVER, DEAL & ROMNEY MARSH
GLASGOW, & PAISLEY
GLOUCESTER, CHELTENHAM
GRAVESEND, DARTFORD
GRAYS, THURROCK
GREAT YARMOUTH, LOWESTOFT
GRIMSBY, CLEETHORPES
GUILDFORD, WOKING
HARLOW, BISHOPS STORTFORD
HARROGATE, KNARESBOROUGH
HASTINGS, BEXHILL, RYE
HEREFORD
HERTFORD, HODDESDON, WARE
HIGH WYCOMBE
HUNTINGDON, ST. NEOTS
IPSWICH, FELIXSTOWE
ISLE OF MAN
ISLE OF WIGHT TOWNS
KENDAL
KIDDERMINSTER
KINGSTON-UPON-HULL
LANCASTER, MORECAMBE
LEICESTER, LOUGHBOROUGH
LINCOLN
LLANDUDNO, COLWYN BAY
LUTON, DUNSTABLE
MACCLESFIELD
MAIDSTONE
MANSFIELD, MANSFIELD WOODHOUSE
MEDWAY, GILLINGHAM
MILTON KEYNES
NEW FOREST TOWNS
NEWBURY, THATCHAM
NEWPORT, CHEPSTOW
NEWQUAY
NEWTOWN, WELSHPOOL
NORTHAMPTON
NORTHWICH, WINSFORD
NORWICH
NOTTINGHAM, EASTWOOD, HUCKNALL, ILKESTON
NUNEATON, BEDWORTH
OXFORD, ABINGDON
PENZANCE, ST. IVES
PETERBOROUGH
PLYMOUTH, IVYBRIDGE, SALTASH, TORPOINT
PORTSMOUTH, HAVANT, WATERLOOVILLE
READING
REDDITCH, BROMSGROVE

REIGATE, BANSTEAD, LEATHERHEAD, DORKING
RHYL, PRESTATYN
RUGBY
ST. ALBANS, WELWYN, HATFIELD
ST. AUSTELL
SALISBURY, AMESBURY, WILTON
SCUNTHORPE
SEVENOAKS
SHREWSBURY
SITTINGBOURNE, FAVERSHAM, ISLE OF SHEPPEY
SLOUGH, MAIDENHEAD, WINDSOR
SOUTHAMPTON, EASTLEIGH
SOUTHEND-ON-SEA
STAFFORD
STEVENAGE, HITCHIN, LETCHWORTH
STIRLING
STOKE-ON-TRENT
STROUD, NAILSWORTH
SWANSEA, NEATH, PORT TALBOT
SWINDON, CHIPPENHAM, MARLBOROUGH
TAUNTON, BRIDGWATER
TELFORD
THANET, CANTERBURY, HERNE BAY, WHITSTABLE
TORBAY (Torquay, Paignton, Newton Abbot)
TRURO, FALMOUTH
TUNBRIDGE WELLS, TONBRIDGE, CROWBOROUGH
WARWICK, ROYAL LEAMINGTON SPA &
    STRATFORD UPON AVON
WATFORD, HEMEL HEMPSTEAD
WELLINGBOROUGH
WESTON-SUPER-MARE, CLEVEDON
WEYMOUTH, DORCHESTER
WINCHESTER, NEW ARLESFORD
WORCESTER, DROITWICH
WORTHING, LITTLEHAMPTON, ARUNDEL
WREXHAM
YORK

COUNTY RED BOOKS (Town Centre Maps)

BEDFORDSHIRE
BERKSHIRE
BUCKINGHAMSHIRE
CAMBRIDGESHIRE
CHESHIRE
CORNWALL
DERBYSHIRE
DEVON
DORSET
ESSEX
GLOUCESTERSHIRE
HAMPSHIRE
HEREFORDSHIRE
HERTFORDSHIRE
KENT
LEICESTERSHIRE & RUTLAND
LINCOLNSHIRE
NORFOLK
NORTHAMPTONSHIRE
NOTTINGHAMSHIRE
OXFORDSHIRE
SHROPSHIRE
SOMERSET
STAFFORDSHIRE
SUFFOLK
SURREY
SUSSEX (EAST)
SUSSEX (WEST)
WILTSHIRE
WORCESTERSHIRE

OTHER MAPS

KENT TO CORNWALL (1:460,000)
CHINA (1:6,000,000)
INDIA (1:3,750,000)
INDONESIA (1:4,000,000)
NEPAL (1,800,000)
SOUTH EAST ASIA (1:6,000,000)
THAILAND (1:1,600,000)

STREET PLANS

CARDIFF
EDINBURGH TOURIST PLAN
ST. ALBANS
WOLVERHAMPTON

OFFICIAL TOURIST & LEISURE MAPS

SOUTH EAST ENGLAND (1:200,000)
KENT & EAST SUSSEX (1:150,000)
SUSSEX & SURREY (1:150,000)
SUSSEX (1:50,000)
SOUTHERN ENGLAND (1:200,000)
ISLE OF WIGHT (1:50,000)
WESSEX (1:200,000)
DORSET (1:150,000)
DEVON & CORNWALL (1:200,000)
CORNWALL (1:180,000)
DEVON (1:200,000)
DARTMOOR & SOUTH DEVON COAST (1:100,000)
EXMOOR & NORTH DEVON COAST (1:100,000)
GREATER LONDON M25 (1:80,000)
EAST ANGLIA (1:200,000)
CHILTERNS & THAMES VALLEY (1:200,000)
THE COTSWOLDS (1:110,000)
COTSWOLDS & SEVERN VALLEY (1:200,000)
WALES (1:250,000)
THE SHIRES OF MIDDLE ENGLAND (1:250,000)
THE MID SHIRES (Staffs, Shrops, etc.) (1:200,000)
PEAK DISTRICT (1:100,000)
SNOWDONIA (1:125,000)
YORKSHIRE (1:200,000)
YORKSHIRE DALES (1:125,000)
NORTH YORKSHIRE MOORS (1:125,000)
NORTH WEST ENGLAND (1:200,000)
ISLE OF MAN (1:60,000)
NORTH PENNINES & LAKES (1:200,000)
LAKE DISTRICT (1:75,000)
BORDERS OF ENGLAND & SCOTLAND (1:200,000)
BURNS COUNTRY (1:200,000)
HEART OF SCOTLAND (1:200,000)
GREATER GLASGOW (1:150,000)
EDINBURGH & THE LOTHIANS (1:150,000)
ISLE OF ARRAN (1:63,360)
FIFE (1:100,000)
LOCH LOMOND & TROSSACHS (1:150,000)
ARGYLL THE ISLES & LOCH LOMOND (1:275,000)
PERTHSHIRE, DUNDEE & ANGUS (1:150,000)
FORT WILLIAM, BEN NEVIS, GLEN COE (1:185,000)
IONA (1:10,000) & MULL (1:115,000)
GRAMPIAN HIGHLANDS (1:185,000)
LOCH NESS & INVERNESS (1:150,000)
SKYE & LOCHALSH (1:130,000)
ARGYLL & THE ISLES (1:200,000)
CAITHNESS & SUTHERLAND (1:185,000)
HIGHLANDS OF SCOTLAND (1:275,000)
WESTERN ISLES (1:125,000)
ORKNEY & SHETLAND (1:128,000)
ENGLAND & WALES (1:650,000)
SCOTLAND (1:500,000)
HISTORIC SCOTLAND (1:500,000)
SCOTLAND CLAN MAP (1:625,000)
BRITISH ISLES (1:1,100,000)
GREAT BRITAIN (1:1,100,000)

EUROPEAN LEISURE MAPS

EUROPE (1:3,100,000)
BENELUX (1:600,000)
FRANCE (1:1,000,000)
GERMANY (1:1,000,000
IRELAND (1:625,000)
ITALY (1:1,000,000)
SPAIN & PORTUGAL (1,1,000,000)
CROSS CHANNEL VISITORS' MAP (1:530,000)
WORLD (1:35,000,000)
WORLD FLAT

TOWNS IN NORTHERN FRANCE STREET ATLAS
BOULOGNE SHOPPERS MAP
CALAIS SHOPPERS MAP
DIEPPE SHOPPERS MAP

ESTATE PUBLICATIONS are also
Distributors in the UK for:

INTERNATIONAL TRAVEL MAPS, Canada
HALLWAG, Switzerland
ORDNANCE SURVEY

Catalogue and prices from:
ESTATE PUBLICATIONS
Bridewell House, Tenterden, Kent. TN30 6EP.
Tel: 01580 764225   Fax: 01580 763720
www.estate-publications.co.uk